Let's Not Age

Let's Just Marinate

LET'S NOT AGE, LET'S JUST MARINATE

Summersdale Publishers Ltd
46 West Street
Chichester
West Sussex
PO19 1RP
UK

www.summersdale.com

Printed in the Czech Republic

ISBN: 978-1-84953-209-9

Disclaimer
Some content included in this book has been published previously in Older, Wiser... Sexier (Summersdale Publishers Ltd, 2010)

Substantial discounts on bulk quantities of Summersdale books are available to corporations, professional associations and other organisations. For details contact Summersdale Publishers by telephone: +44 (0) 1243 771107, fax: +44 (0) 1243 786300 or email: nicky@summersdale.com.

Let's Not Age

Let's Just Marinate

Bev Williams

summersdale

When I'm old and grey, I want to have a house by the sea... with a lot of wonderful chums, good music and booze around.

Ava Gardner

I'm like old wine. They don't bring me out very often, but I'm well preserved.

Rose Fitzgerald Kennedy

Always travel first class –

or your children will.

Nobody loves life like he
who is growing old.

Sophocles

One should never make one's debut
in a scandal. One should reserve
that to give interest to one's old age.

Oscar Wilde

We only have one regret at our age,

and that's all the sins
we didn't commit.

The young man knows the rules but the old man knows the exceptions.

Oliver Wendell Holmes

My rule of life prescribed as an absolutely sacred rite smoking cigars and also the drinking of alcohol before, after and if need be during all meals and in the intervals between them.

Winston Churchill

On the whole, the years have
been kind to us all –

it was just the weekends
which did the damage.

If I had my life to live over again, I'd make the same mistakes, only sooner.

Tallulah Bankhead

They say that age is all in your mind. The trick is keeping it from creeping down into your body.

Anonymous

We might be older,

but nobody said we were wiser.

I'd hate to die with a good liver... when I die I want everything to be knackered.

Hamish Imlach

Now I'm getting older I don't need to do drugs any more. I can get the same effect just by standing up real fast.

Jonathan Katz

Let's not age,

lets just marinate.

Every day I beat my own
previous record for the number of
consecutive days I've stayed alive.

George Carlin

You're only as young as the last
time you changed your mind.

Timothy Leary

If in doubt –

add more wine.

Old age likes indecency.
It's a sign of life.

Mason Cooley

Live for the moment...

and never dance with boring people.

Stay busy, get plenty of exercise, and don't drink too much. Then again, don't drink too little.

Herman Smith-Johannsen

I keep fit. Every morning, I do a hundred laps of an Olympic-sized swimming pool – in a small motor launch.

Peter Cook

Growing older is a dream come true.

You can't see what's irritating you.

The secret of genius is to carry the spirit of the child into old age.

Aldous Huxley

Don't let ageing get you down. It's too hard to get back up.

John Wagner

You read about the dangers of
alcohol so you better give up...

reading.

The ageing process has you firmly in its grasp if you never get the urge to throw a snowball.

Doug Larson

You don't get older, you get better.

Shirley Bassey

Whatever your age, adventures
are good for you –

so blow out your candles.

A man ought to get drunk at least twice a year... so he won't let himself get snotty about it.

Raymond Chandler

Once, during Prohibition, I was forced to live for days on nothing but food and water.

W. C. Fields

The best way to enjoy yourself –

is very, very, very... badly.

With mirth and laughter
let old wrinkles come.

William Shakespeare,
The Merchant of Venice

While there's snow on the roof,
it doesn't mean the fire has
gone out in the furnace.

John G. Diefenbaker

At your age people expect you to
be calm, dignified and sober.

Disappoint them.

Since I got to be sixty-five, I look better, feel better, make love better and I never lied better.

George Burns

Just when you've learned to make the most of your life -

you wonder where most of your life has gone.

I envy people who drink –
at least they know what to
blame everything on.

Oscar Levant

When people are old enough
to know better, they're old
enough to do worse.

Hesketh Pearson

If God had meant me
to touch my toes -

he would have put
chocolates on the floor.

Birthdays are good for you.
Statistics show that the people who
have the most live the longest.

Larry Lorenzoni

You only live once, but if you
do it right, once is enough.

Mae West

Older, wiser...

sexier.

One of the best parts of growing older? You can flirt all you like since you've become harmless.

Liz Smith

I believe in loyalty; I think when a woman reaches an age she likes she should stick to it.

Eva Gabor

No wise man ever wished
to be younger.

Jonathan Swift

Wrinkles should merely indicate
where smiles have been.

Mark Twain

Eventually you will reach a point when you stop lying about your age and start bragging about it.

Will Rogers

My grandmother is over eighty and still doesn't need glasses. Drinks right out of the bottle.

Henny Youngman

We grow quieter as we grow older.

Must be because we have a
lot to be quiet about.

If you obey all the rules,
you miss all the fun.

Katharine Hepburn

Youth is a disease from
which we all recover.

Dorothy Fuldheim

Laughter doesn't require teeth.

Bill Newton

Never eat healthy food.

We need all the
preservatives we can get.

You're only young once, but
you can be immature forever.

John Greier

I have taken more out of alcohol
than alcohol has taken out of me.

Winston Churchill

Feeling older...

is for sissies!

It's not how old you are,
it's how you are old.

Brian Blessed

There comes a time in every
woman's life when the only thing
that helps is a glass of champagne.

Bette Davis

Is it time for your medication –

or mine?

I just tell people I'm as old as my wife. Then I lie about her age.

Fred Metcalf

An advanced old woman is uncontrollable by any earthly force.

Dorothy L. Sayers

I'm a multi-tasker.

I go to parties, I smile, I talk, I enjoy great food and I have little drinkies.

We do not stop playing because
we grow old. We grow old
because we stop playing!

Benjamin Franklin

How pleasant is the day
when we give up striving to
be young – or slender.

William James

Back in the sixties we turned
on, tuned in and dropped out.

Now we tune in, turn
over and drop off.

Just remember, once you're over the hill, you begin to pick up speed.

Charles M. Schulz

'We never argue.

We can't hear each other.'

Don't act your age. Act like
the inner young person
you have always been.

J. A. West

The only form of exercise
I take is massage.

Truman Capote

Sometimes we deserve champagne.

Sometimes we need it.

The age of a woman doesn't mean a thing. The best tunes are played on the oldest fiddles.

Ralph Waldo Emerson

To stop ageing – keep on raging.

Michael Forbes

It's a huge responsibility...

being the ultimate fantasy pin-up.

Brandy, n. A cordial composed of one part thunder-and-lightning, one part remorse, two parts bloody murder, one part death-hell-and-the-grave and four parts clarified Satan.

Ambrose Bierce

A drink a day keeps the shrink away.

Edward Abbey

Women love silent men –

they think they're listening.

No man is ever old enough
to know better.

Holbrook Jackson

Old age is an excellent time
for outrage. My goal is to say
or do at least one outrageous
thing every week.

Maggie Kuhn

Growing older is hard enough –

without having to act it.

We learn from experience that men never learn anything from experience.

George Bernard Shaw

It's OK to have sex after a heart attack. But don't forget to close the ambulance door.

Phyllis Diller

Growing older?

No – you just need repotting.

Teetotallers lack
the sympathy and
generosity of men
that drink.

W. H. Davies

We have great respect for maturity...

especially if it's in a bottle!

They tell you that you'll lose your mind when you grow older. What they don't tell you is that you won't miss it very much.

Malcolm Cowley

I had a muscle that twitched all day yesterday. It's the most exercise I've had in years.

Terry Martin

Both you and the wine
improve with age –

and the more you age,
the more we love you.

I know I'm drinking
myself to a slow death, but
then I'm in no hurry.

Robert Benchley

I like to give my inhibitions
a bath now and then.

Oliver Reed

Just how naughty can we be –

and still go to heaven?

I have never known a person
live to be one hundred and be
remarkable for anything else.

Josh Billings

I complain that the years fly
past, but then I look in the
mirror and see that very few
of them actually got past.

Robert Brault

You know you are getting older when

people ring at 8 p.m. asking
'Did I wake you?'

You really haven't changed
in seventy or eighty years.
Your body changes, but
you don't change at all.

Doris Lessing

The hands of my biological clock
are giving me the finger.

Wendy Liebman

Age?

Why would we lie about
a thing like that?

It's a good idea to obey all the
rules when you're young just
so you'll have the strength to
break them when you're old.

Mark Twain

A man's only as old as
the woman he feels.

Groucho Marx

When a recipe says 'add wine' –

never ask 'to what?'.

People say I'm into my second childhood. The reality is that I never left my first one.

Spike Milligan

Funny how a little age

can add flavour.

Then trust me there's
nothing like drinking,
So pleasant on this
side of the grave:
It keeps the unhappy
from thinking,
And makes e'en the
valiant more brave.

Charles Dibdin

Let us be lazy in everything,
except in loving and drinking.

Gotthold Ephraim Lessing

Save water –

drink wine.

www.summersdale.com

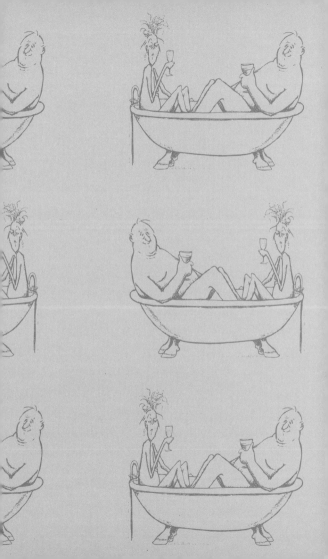

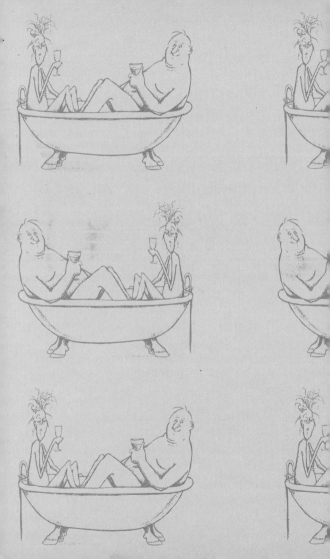

Dear Joey,

You are a wonderful person & I treasure our friendship.

xoxo
Britt